Finally Making Money

Published by Peoples Church Network

PEOPLES
CHURCH
NETWORK

ISBN: 978-0-578-91081-9

Artwork: A.M.Frasier

To Brandon II, Isaiah, and Keilah.

You are the greatest gift God has given us!

Thank you for being so outstanding in everything.

Intro

Congratulations! We're serious about that! You have done something that most people who grow up poor cannot do - escape poverty. According to the National Center for Children in Poverty, "children who grow up poor are more likely to be poor as adults."[2] The fact that you are making enough money to do more than just live check to check is huge! Whether it's because you've been working your butt off for years at your job and they've finally given you the promotion you deserved or you have been grinding it out at college and now you've got the job of your dreams, the fact is, you've made it! So, take a second to pat yourself on the back. You might even want to look at your checking account, pay stub, or offer letter that lets you know you made it and soak in the reality that things are looking good right now.

We, Brandon and my wife, Dorothy ("Dot"), both know that feeling. We grew up in Toledo, Ohio with our parents struggling to keep food on the table and a roof over our heads. We met each other as teenagers and bonded because we both were committed to getting out of Toledo and leaving poverty behind. The story of our success is based on our commitment to each other and our faith in Jesus. Our understanding of how difficult it can be to break out of poverty and know how to manage money has resulted from years of education and life experienc-

2 www.nccp.org/publications/pub 911.html

es, considering we never had money, and even more, never knew anyone else who had it either. We have used that experience to coach and train many people to easily manage their finances, whether they make hundreds or thousands per week. All with the goal of turning their money into wealth so they can enjoy life now and set up their children for financial success as well.

This book is going to teach you a few basic principles and practices that you will be able to utilize right away. We will use some stories from our lives so you can see how those principles play out in real life and we will provide some useful tools to help you along in your financial journey. We learned a great deal of what we know from mentors and by trial and error, so we understand that money management is not easy. However, we also know that if someone had taught us the things we are going to share with you earlier in our lives, we would not have had to learn the hard way and would have experienced even more financial success than we have achieved now. Experience is the teacher of fools! You should not have to experience the pitfalls of poor money management because we have already done that for you and you likely have seen others who have done the same. If you follow the principles and use the tools we provide, you will have everything you need to manage your financial resources well and to begin building wealth.

"The right tool for the job."

Money Is A Tool

Having a proper perspective of money

The very first thing you need to handle your money well is the proper perspective of money. There is a good chance that your perspective of money has been warped, like ours was, due to the many poor influences you had in life. As children, we watched our parents celebrate when they got money or mourn when money was lacking. There were, and still are, shows on TV that portray rich people without a reasonable care in the world and poor people with way too many cares. In the 80s and 90s, when we were young, there was a show called *Lifestyles of The Rich and Famous* (the predecessor to MTV's show, *Cribs*) that helped us imagine that money equals happiness. In music, especially hip-hop music, money is the central theme of so many songs – whether already having or striving to get money. It is so pervasive that many people in poverty who listen to that kind of music automatically become emotionally attached to money. All these influences lead us to attach our emotional well-being to money, which is totally incorrect. Money should not dictate your emotions! You are smart enough to know this, but everything around you tells you differently.

So, let's set the record straight: the proper perspective is to see money as a tool. Just like a hammer, screwdriver, or saw. It is a tool that you use to buy things you need and/or want. When we moved into our home, we knew immediately that we would need to do some renovations. We wanted an "open concept" home where you can pretty much see the whole first floor from the kitchen so that we could host a large group of people from our church, when needed, without everyone being divided up into separate rooms. To make that happen, we needed to do some major demolition and construction, which included tearing down a wall. We are not the type of people to pay someone to do something we could possibly do on our own, which is a very good way to save a lot of money. But in order to do this, we knew we would need the right tools. We needed an electric saw, a sledge-hammer, and a nail gun, to name a few that are not normal household tools. First, we had to acquire these tools. Then, we had to learn how to use them in order to achieve our goal. Once we did all of that, we then were able to complete our renovation beautifully.

> ***...THE PROPER PERSPECTIVE IS TO SEE MONEY AS A TOOL.***

We now have learned to see money just like the tools we needed to renovate our home. We had no emotional attachment to the tools we used. We didn't cry when we did not have a reciprocating saw, nor did we celebrate when we had a hammer drill; they were simply objects we used to accomplish our goal. We also did not start the renovation until we had the tools we *thought* we needed. At times we had to stop in the middle of doing something because we learned we did not have the right tool.

Our emotional attachment was to the things we could do once we finished the renovation, never on the tools used for the renovation. You need to learn to see money in the same way. You sometimes need to acquire it to accomplish some things, but it should not be the object of your desire. Focus on and attach your emotional energy to the thing you want to accomplish or do, not the tool. There will be times when you cannot do something because you don't have the money, just like when we had to stop our renovation because we didn't have the right tool. That's hard, we know, but that is life! If the thing you want is important enough, then it's worth waiting for and you will enjoy it even more when you have the right tools.

Could Be Dangerous

Almost any tool, when used improperly, has the potential to be dangerous. Our decision to renovate our new home was not a spur of the moment decision. This was our third home purchase and we had renovated the basements of our last two homes, so we had gained enough experience to feel comfortable tackling this project. However, when renovating our first basement, we had a friend helping us who was just as inexperienced as we were. We purchased a miter saw (which is a circular saw mounted to a lever) so that we could make the work go faster. The miter saw is a very useful tool when used properly, but it can cause some permanent damage when not used correctly. Well, our friend decided to cut a piece of wood that was too small, and the saw snatched the wood and his - finger - into the blade! Fortunately, the wood jammed itself into the saw and stopped the blade from cutting our friend's finger completely off. This same principal applies to money. When used properly, it is an outstanding tool, but if used incorrectly, it is very dangerous.

Some quick examples of using money improperly are:

> 1. *Borrowing money for things that do not gain value or help us earn money*
>
> 2. *Spending money to make us "feel better"*
>
> 3. *Not knowing how much money we have*
>
> 4. *Being short sighted with money as opposed to preparing for the future*
>
> 5. *Loaning money to family and friends that we cannot afford to lose*

All these things (and many others) are ways that people use money totally wrong and end up hurting themselves and others in the process. If money is not used correctly, you can end up in a much worse situation than being poor. Many people end up in debt to people, the bank, or the government, which can lead to being dependent on others and destitute for the rest of their lives. You can avoid all of this by allowing the fact that money is just a tool to sink deeply into your understanding and by making a commitment to use that tool properly.

If you're wondering if we are trying to scare you a bit, you're kind of right. However, instead of thinking of this as a scare tactic, think of it as us helping you gain a proper respect for an extremely powerful tool. We do not want you to be afraid to use money, we want quite the opposite. We want you to use money for all that it's worth. Just keep the proper perspective and respect for the tool you are using.

Get Over Your Fear

One of the most important tools we had when doing our renovation was the nail gun. If you have never used one, it's just like it sounds. It is a heavy, awkward gun that shoots nails instead of bullets. This was not Dot's favorite tool to use because it was heavy and potentially dangerous if there were any mistakes in how it was used. I completely understood her hesitation, but the fact was that if we wanted to get the renovation done, she was going to need to get past her fear and work with the nail gun. After some practice and a few fixable mistakes, she overcame her fear, and we were able to get the job done.

In the same way, you will need to overcome your fear of money in order to use it correctly. We know what you are thinking: "I'm not scared of money!" Of course, you are not physically afraid of the green paper or round coins, but we are willing to bet that you are afraid of not having money, afraid of what happens if you misuse it, or you fear tracking your money. If you did not have one of those fears, then you probably would not be reading this book. So, let's put those first two fears of not having money and of misusing money to bed. Once you finish reading this book and begin following our practices, you will no longer have to worry about them. However, you will need to tackle your fear of tracking your money head-on if that is a problem.

> ***...KEEPING TRACK OF YOUR MONEY WILL DECREASE YOUR STRESS AND ALLOW YOU TO SPEND WITHOUT GUILT.***

To manage your money effectively, you need to know how much is coming in and going out - down to the penny. Yep, you heard us. If you are not willing to manage your money down to the penny, you will, sooner or later, have a difficult time tracking your nickels, dimes, quarters, and dollars. Sometimes, this fear comes from not knowing how to track your money, fearing that if you track your money, it will stress you out, or, once you do start keeping track, it will limit your spending or fun. All of these fears come from lies that we have told ourselves or heard from others. The truth is that keeping track of your money will decrease your stress, allow you to spend without guilt, and therefore have more fun. We are going to help you with knowing how to track your spending in the next chapter. So, if you have avoided tracking your money because you are not sure how, take a deep breath...maybe get a glass of water and get ready to learn how easy it is going to be to track your money, a.k.a., make a budget.

"Budgeting...it isn't rocket science"

Gotta Budget

It's easier than you think

If money is a tool, then the budget is the instruction manual.

There are two types of people in the world: those who will take a set of instructions and read them carefully, making sure to follow them to the letter, and then, there are people who don't even bother to acknowledge that instructions exist. We tend to be instructions people. Yes, there are times when we skim through the instructions quickly and other times when we read them word for word. But as a whole, we know that someone has taken a great deal of time, effort, and expense to write them - so they are usually worth a look.

During the span of our decades of marriage, we have purchased a great deal of furniture that required a bit of assembly. Our last adventure included putting together three full length, floor to ceiling, wardrobes from IKEA. We had heard the jokes about people hating putting together IKEA furniture and we had watched the DIY television shows with couples almost getting divorced after an argument that occurred over IKEA furniture. For us, it was a totally different experience. We were able to put these wardrobes together in a couple of hours and even had fun in the process. Our experience was not different from others because we have some supernatural Swedish furniture building skills, it was because we carefully read and followed the instructions. We made sure we had all the pieces, set everything out in an open area, and looked at every step to completion *before* we started assembling so that we had a general idea of how things were to go together - just as the instructions told us. As a result, we saved ourselves a great deal of time, money, and stress. Every time we have a friend tell us they don't like self-assembly furniture we ask, "Do you follow the instructions?" Almost every time the answer is, "No." The moral of the story is if you prepare to follow and then follow the instructions, you will have success.

These same things apply to using a budget. So, what type of person are you? If you know that you are not the type to read the instructions, then making and following a budget might be a bit of a challenge for you, but you have overcome challenges before. That is how you've reached the level of success you have experienced up to this point, and it is going to be the key to your success going forward. You can do this!

If you are an instruction person, you are ahead of the game, and chances are you just need to learn how to put a budget together.

Now, here is the 100% truth: If you don't have a budget, you will, at best, struggle managing your money and will have a hard time getting by on a daily basis. At worst (and most likely), you will end up in a great deal of debt and falling back into poverty because you mismanaged the money that you have now. You also will screw up your chances of having your money build wealth for you in the future. So, if you are not willing to take the time and the small amount of effort needed to make a basic budget for you and your family (present or future), save yourself some time and don't bother reading the rest of this book. You wasted your money buying this just as you will likely waste your money going forward until you get a budget.

However, if you are ready and willing to break the

chains of poverty and take your finances to the next level, then let's get started.

30-Day Challenge

Making a budget is easy! You do not need to be an accountant or math whiz. You just need to know how to count money. The first step is counting all the money you spend over the next 30 days. Wait, we know what you are thinking. You're thinking, "I thought you said this was going to be easy!" And you're right, we said it would be easy, we did not say it was going to be fast. Has anything with life-long impact ever happened quickly? It takes 40 weeks to have a baby, and about a year to plan a dream wedding; both of those things have life-long impacts for you. Learning how to make and follow a budget will be almost as valuable, so tracking your spending for the next month is a relatively short amount of time considering the rest of your life.

The best way for you to track your spending is to keep your receipts for everything - every trip to the store, every fast-food stop, every gas purchase. Have a place in your car, purse, or bag where you keep them, and just drop your receipts in that same spot every time you make a purchase.

Be sure that you print out receipts from on-line purchases and any automatic payments that you have set-up via credit cards or from your bank account. No matter how you spend your money, make sure that you are able to keep track of every penny for the next month. If you share expenses with anyone, such as a spouse or significant other, make sure they are doing the same. For your budget to work, you need to know exactly how much money you spend, as a unit, on a monthly basis.

We recommend that you write all of these expenses out on a daily basis - yes with old school paper and pencil! This is going to take some extra effort, but if you have sworn off the use of paper, you can use an app or a spreadsheet on your tablet or computer. If your life is hectic, then it is fine if you write them out two or three times a week. The date you make the purchase is not that important, only the amount and what you bought. If you need to make a note on the receipt to remind yourself the purpose of the purchase, be sure to do that. To help you with keeping track of your spending, we put together this basic spreadsheet (see Appendix A or if you have the workbook you can keep track there). If you need more than one sheet, that's fine, use as many as you need to capture all of your expenses for the month. We strongly suggest that you write this information out by hand, but if you are using a computer, you may find an even better spreadsheet template to use or find an app on your phone or tablet. It doesn't matter what you use as long as you keep track and are able to put your purchases in the categories we outline below.

On our spreadsheet we have broken down the expenses into the following 13 categories:

Housing - *Rent, Mortgage, Property taxes, Insurance, etc.*

Transportation - *Car payment, Gas, Bus, Insurance, Repairs, etc.*

Utilities - *Gas, Oil, Electric, Water, etc.*

Telephone - *Home phone, Cell phone*

Groceries - *Everything bought from the store - food, toiletries, etc.*

Dining, Travel, Entertainment - *Restaurant food, Vacation, Cable, Netflix, memberships, etc.*

Debt Payments - *Credit card bill, School loans, etc.*

Education - *School fees, Daycare, Uniforms, etc.*

Charity - *Tithes, Offerings, other cash donations*

Savings - *Money put aside for future use*

Clothing - *Clothes, shoes, and accessories*

Medical - *Insurance not taken out of your check, Copays, Medicine, etc.*

Miscellaneous - *Child support, Hair dresser, etc. Anything that does not fit into other categories*

We have found that 90% of most peoples' expenses fall into the first 12 areas and we have the miscellaneous category to catch everything else. For you to manage your money well, you need to know where it is being spent. Once you complete the 30-day challenge, you will know exactly where you are spending. So, do yourself a favor; resist the urge to toss everything into the miscellaneous category. It's very tempting to do and even we get lazy and use that when we don't remember what we purchased and didn't make a note of it. But starting out, you must be accurate for this to work.

Pay Yo' Bills! Please!

This should go without saying, but we have had so many people make this mistake that we would be doing you a disservice if we didn't mention that it is very important for you to pay your bills - in full! We understand that when growing up in poverty, we sometimes must prioritize bills and skip paying some in order to pay the most important ones. It's a survival technique and honestly, we don't fault people for working their system that way. However, now that you have the financial means to cover all your expenses, PAY YO' BILLS!! You have broken the cycle of poverty, now you need to break the habits of poverty.

You no longer should pay the minimum amount needed to keep your lights, gas, cable, etc. from getting cut off just so you can have "extra" cash. That was only acceptable when there was no extra cash. Now that you have it, pay your bills off completely, every month. The full amount of these bills is exactly what you need to record in your 30-day challenge, not the minimum. To begin to build wealth, you must start from a place of no debt and that includes your regular monthly bills. We will talk more about debt later in the book, but as you walk through the 30-day challenge, we want to make sure this is clear.

Bills include special taxes too...

If you are an entrepreneur, that is great, but make sure you are paying your quarterly income taxes. If you are a business owner and you don't know what we are talking about, then you need to find an accountant and ask them to help you plan for your taxes right now! If your state requires personal property taxes, make sure you pay those as well. Plan on that bill coming every year.

The Good Part!

The second part of the 30-day challenge is way easier than the first, and more fun! This is the part where you calculate and keep track of how much money you make. Basically, you just need to count your money; and if you don't like counting your money then you first need to check your pulse to make sure you're still alive. The key thing here is that we are only counting the money you bring home. In accounting, it's called your "net income." We just say it's the money that actually makes it into your home or bank account. At this time, we don't even count the money placed in work savings/investment plans such as a 401k or Simple IRA. If it is taken out of your check before you get it (taxes, health insurance, etc.), then do not count it as income here, just to keep it simple.

Chances are you have only one source of income and

that is your job. That's what makes this part easy. If you have multiple jobs or sources of consistent income, then you need to add those sources of income together to figure out how much money you bring home on a monthly basis. You want to make sure you are only counting the money that you know will be coming in on a ***consistent basis***; every month guaranteed, unless something tragic happens. We understand that sometimes extra money comes in from time to time. Maybe you have a side hustle that brings in a little extra cash here and there. That's fine, but for the purposes of making a budget, you have to act like that doesn't even exist. That includes if you are fortunate enough to get tax return money. Do not include that return in your budget right now. All those things we will count as extra money and we will talk about how to handle that later.

YOU HAVE BROKEN THE CYCLE OF POVERTY, NOW YOU NEED TO BREAK THE HABITS OF POVERTY.

Now back to counting your money (ie. consistent income). If you are salaried, meaning you work for a set amount that does not change based on the number of hours you work or you work a very constant schedule, then you probably already know how much money you bring home on a weekly, bi-weekly, or monthly basis. If you are paid monthly (or twice a month totaling 24 checks a year), write the amount you bring home every month in the space marked "Average Monthly Income" on the spreadsheet (Appendix A or workbook) and you are done. If you are paid weekly or bi-weekly, you need to do a little math.

If you are paid weekly, take the amount you make and multiply it by 52. Which will give you the total amount you will bring home every year because you will get 52 checks in a year. Then take that number and divided it by 12 (because there are 12 months in a year). You now have the amount of money you bring home per month. Take that number and write it down on the spreadsheet. Here's an example:

Your weekly check is $750*

$750 x 52 (weeks in a year) =

$39,000 per year

$39,000/12 (months in a year) =

$3250 per month

*Remember, this is what you take home and have access to immediately.

If you are paid bi-weekly and get a total of 26 checks a year, you will need to take the amount you took home from your last check and multiply that by 26, which will give you the amount you bring home per year. And then divide that amount by 12 to get the amount of money you bring home per month. This is an average amount you will bring home per month over the course of a year. Ten months of the year you will bring home two checks which means your actual amount will be less than your yearly average. However, two months of the year you will bring home three checks and have more than your average. IMPORTANT: On those three check months, do not act like you got extra money! No. No. No! That third check has already been accounted for in your budget. Stick to the same budget all the time. Check out the sample below:

Your bi-weekly check is $1625

$1625 x 26 = $42,250 per year

$42,250/12 = **$3520.83** per month

If you're hourly and paid weekly, you will need to average your paycheck from the last 4 weeks and then multiply by 52 and divide by 12. If your hours are variable, it's OK, that's why we are calculating the average. Check the sample below:

From your last four checks, you took home: $845, $763, $772, $743.

Add them together: $845+$763+$772+$743 = $3123

Divide the total by 4: $3123/4 = $780.75 (Average weekly take home amount)

Multiply by 52: $780.75 x 52 = $40,599 (Yearly take home pay)

Divide by 12: $40,599/12 = **$3,383.25** (Average Monthly Income)

Write your Average Monthly Income in the space provided on the spreadsheet.

If you're paid by contract, then you will need to either estimate the amount you make per month by looking at how much you made last year and dividing it by 12 or you can look at the contracts you have this year and calculate your monthly income from that. However, you will need to account for taxes. Depending on the amount of money made your taxes could be higher or lower than previous years. We suggest you talk to an accountant to estimate your taxes. If you have worked as a contractor for some time, and your income is close to last years, you can use the amount of taxes you paid last year as an estimate of what you will pay this year. Either way, be sure to account for taxes when calculating how much you will actually pocket from your income.

Now that you have your monthly income, you will be ready to make your budget as soon as you track all your spending for the month. So, this is what you need to do: Mark this next "Build Your Budget" section so that after you finish the 30-day challenge, you can come back to it and complete your budget. **THIS IS ESSENTIAL!** We want you to finish reading the book now so that you can get all the other information, but if you don't come back and put your budget together, you are setting up yourself for failure. So, go on to the next section starting on page 41, for now, and then come back to this later.

START HERE AFTER COMPLETING THE 30 DAY CHALLENGE

So, you came back! Excellent, you are a Rock Star... or you like not being broke!

Build Your Budget

As we said before, money is just a tool. It is a very powerful tool, but nothing more than a tool. Your budget is the instructions for using that tool. The first time we put a budget together as a couple, it was out of desperation. We lived in a two-bedroom apartment with two cars, standard utility payments, and some credit card debt because we thought it would be smart to pay for our wedding using the Discover Card we acquired in college. It was not smart at all! To top that off, we decided to reward ourselves by purchasing a brand-new car upon my, Brandon's, graduation. Just to set the record straight, we bought Brandon a new car with a copy of his degree and a job offer letter and the car dealer let us! That likely would not happen now. Note: Lenders and salespeople are not your friends! They have motives and business goals behind their kindness and apparent generosity when giving discounts and deals.

Anyway, after buying the car and signing the lease on the apartment, we calculated our income, subtracted our expenses and had almost nothing left over at the end of the month. We were barely just getting by and the quick income minus expense calculation only showed us how bad it was. We quickly learned that it is better to figure out whether we can afford something before buying it! We should have waited to buy the car.

We then went through the process that we are about to share with you. We put a plan together to decide how we were going to spend our money going forward to avoid the pain of barely getting by. This plan is known as making a budget!

1) Group Spending into Categories

Take all the expenses from your 30-day challenge that have the same category and group them together. All your housing expenses should go together, and then transportation, utilities, etc. You should come up with a total amount spent over the month in each category. Place those totals on the Expense Table.

Example Expense Table		
Categories	**Totals**	**Budget**
Housing (Rent, mortgage, taxes, insurance)	$775.00	
Transportation (Gas, Bus, Car Note, Repairs)	$680.49	
Utilities (Gas, Electric)	$163.39	
Telephone	$78.93	
Groceries	$149.89	
Medical	$0.00	
Dining, travel, entertainment (Including Cable, Netflix)	$248.86	
Debt payments	$125.00	
Clothing/household	$54.89	
Savings	$0.00	
Education	$625.00	
Tithes & Offerings (Donations)	$200.00	
Miscellaneous	$35.69	
Total Expense	**$3,137.14**	

At this point, people are usually shocked at how much money they spend. They are especially shocked that they spend so much in specific categories like Entertainment/Travel or Transportation. When we did this for the first time, we couldn't believe so much money passed through our hands every month. Do not let this discourage you! You are on your way!! Now let's get past the shock and move on to the next step.

2) Subtract your expenses from your income

Add all your expense categories together on the Expense Table to see how much you spent altogether last month. Another opportunity to be shocked, but remember, money is just a tool.

Now, take that number and put it in the "Income Minus Expense" table. Take your monthly income that you calculated from earlier and place it in that same table. Now, subtract your expenses from your income and see what you have left over every month.

Income Minus Expense		
	Current	Budget
Monthly Income	$3,018.65	
Monthly Expenses	$3,137.14	
Total	**($118.49)**	

Don't be shocked if the number you come up with is negative. Negative is not good, but don't let it stress you out.

Chances are you already knew that number was not going to look good. We will help make it look better soon enough. You should let the realization that you spend more money than you make be your motivation to make some changes, because if you continue the path you are on, it will get really ugly very soon!

On the other hand, if your number is positive, that is great! You should feel good about that. However, that does not mean that you are finished. It does mean that you can start building wealth a bit faster, but we have found that people in your situation tend to have a hard time sticking to their budget and before long, end up spending more than they make as well. So, do not skip the next step!

3) Set spending limits for each category

This, our friends, is where we separate the adults from the children. You now need to set some spending limits so that you will never spend more than you make again. Your ability to set these limits and stick to them will determine whether you have financial success or end up in financial ruin.

If you found that you spent less than you made, this process should be easy. Just look at the amount you spent during the month and make some round numbers close to the amount you spent last month. (Round numbers = only whole dollars, don't worry about the change). If you did not put any money into savings, then you want to plan on doing that next month. We will talk more about saving and investing later in the book, but if you don't have some cash set aside for emergencies, you need to place the extra money you have in that area. Also, even though you had enough money to cover your expenses, you should still ask yourself if you can reduce spending in some categories. Ben Franklin said, "A penny saved is a penny earned." And he was right. If you make the choice not to spend on some dining or miscellaneous items, you will have more money available to build wealth.

> ***IF YOU STICK TO YOUR BUDGET YOU WILL FIND THAT YOU NO LONGER HAVE A REASON TO WORRY ABOUT MONEY.***

If you barely had enough income to cover your expenses, then, unfortunately, you are in the same boat as the people who had a negative amount. You both need to set spending limits that will give you enough space to prevent you from getting close to spending more than your income in the future and to allow you to have some money to put away into savings. See the "Sample Budget" sheet (Appendix C). The sample we provided shows how we rounded certain categories up and others we decreased to keep from over-spending the following month. Notice that we left "Housing" exactly as it was because that category is usually the same amount every month, so no need to estimate there. However, "Transportation and Utilities" we rounded up a bit because those expenses will fluctuate with gas prices and temperature. We also decreased amounts in areas such as "Miscellaneous and Dining" to make sure we did not over-spend, but we increased the budget in groceries because if we are not spending as much money at restaurants, we will likely spend more at the grocery store. You see what we are doing, right? Some of the budget is guessing what you will spend and adjusting as needed. We can't tell you what you need to put in every category. For every individual/family, that number is different. However, we can tell you that the final amount of your budget needs to be less than your income.

The spending limits that you put in each category is your budget! See, that wasn't hard at all. You now have the basic instructions on how you should use your money. If you stick to your budget, you will find that you no longer have a reason to worry about money. You won't need to worry about whether you will have anything left at the end of the month or whether your bills will get paid. So many people never go through the process of making a budget and, as a result, never have a sense of peace, financially. You now are on the road to financial stability!

If you find that even with your budget your money is extremely tight because of expenses that cannot easily be changed such as rent, a car note, or utilities, then you have a tough situation, but not an impossible one. It's going to take some sacrifice, but you will find that it is worth it.

1. Get a side hustle to pay down debt

In our example, if that family could earn some extra money and pay down their credit card expenses, they could save an extra $125/mo. That change alone would put them in a position where they could start saving money or putting that extra towards paying off those student loans.

2. Get a roommate or move in with a friend

We know that as an adult, you want a space of your own. Noble idea, but that is not always possible if you're right out of college or haven't reached the financial threshold that allows you to afford a nice place in a good neighborhood. You may only need to do this for a couple of years until you get rid of other expenses, such as debt, that cause you financial problems.

3. Refinance your car/re-quote your insurance

Try to adjust some of your monthly expenses that can be adjusted. If you are paying a high interest rate on your car, try getting that lowered and get the term of your loan extended so that you can pay less per month. DO NOT get the term increased at the same interest rate! You will be paying more. If you have had the same insurance company for over two years and your driving record is good, you should consider getting a new insurance quote.

By making one or more of these changes, you will be able to decrease your expenses and have a decent amount of money left over at the end of the month to feel financially secure and to begin thinking about wealth building. But...what about emergencies, special expenses, or one-time purchases?

One-Time Expenses

The question about one-time purchases comes up quite often because people worry about whether they will be able to buy anything special like a new television or furniture. We have two things to say about these types of expenses:

1. First, if you find that you are making "one-time purchases" every month, then you are likely just spending money on impulse. This is something that you need to recognize, call it what it is, and put it down as a category in your budget. If you plan on impulse buying every month and doing it does not cause your expenses to be more than your income, then there is no financial problem with it. However, if it makes you go over budget, then you must put a quick end to it. Don't worry though, we will have a 100% effective solution in the next chapter.

2. Second, every budget must have a savings category. We placed it in our sample budget because it is key to protecting yourself from unexpected/emergency expenses. You should expect that unplanned things will happen such as your car needing repair or a window getting broken. At some point, you are going to need to call someone to your home to fix something. **THINGS HAPPEN - PLAN FOR**

THEM! This does not need to negatively affect you financially because you will plan for these things to happen by putting money away into savings every month. So, when you get a flat tire, you don't worry about how it's going to affect your finances because you already planned for it in your budget. We encourage you to put $500 away into savings as soon as you can and then add $50 (or more) to it every month depending on your income. If you own your home, put away at least $100 every month and **don't ever touch it** unless there is an emergency. If you go years without a real emergency, thank God and keep on saving. If you own your home, you will eventually need to replace the furnace, roof, or some other expensive thing. If you don't own your home, you can use these savings as a down payment for your future home!!! That's part of building wealth!

As for other special purchases, simply plan for that purchase in your budget by adding a category and putting money away for it every month (most of the time, that will be done in a second savings account). We've had as many as six different savings accounts that we put money into monthly for future "one-time purchases." We have a savings account for travel, gifts, and home renovations to name a few. Basically, if you plan for the purchase, you will be fine, and the budget is the best way for you to plan.

What should I do with my tax return?

Ahh, the tax return. The Christmas after Christmas! We know that tax season for many people is truly the most wonderful time of the year, and we don't want to spoil that for you. We do want to help you use that large amount of money wisely. This advice also should be applied to end-of-year bonuses or any other large amount of money that you received outside of your regular paycheck.

1. *Put some of it in your checking account to act as a financial cushion. If your checking account never drops below $500 a month, you have enough cushion, but more would be better.*

2. *Use it to pay off credit card debt. You will save lots of money on interest charges.*

3. *Use it to build your Emergency Savings of $500.*

4. *If you already have done item numbers 1 – 3, then put 1/2 toward building wealth (see Chapter 5) and spend the other 1/2 on one of those special purchases. Live a little!*

You can have fun and buy nice things while being financially responsible. Just be responsible first, and then have fun!

Now that you have the instructions for how to use your money, we are going to tell you how to stick to those instructions and settle into a habit of never spending over budget.

1. GET A SIDE HUSTLE TO PAY DOWN DEBT.

2. GET A ROOMMATE OF MOVE IN WITH A FRIEND.

3. REFINANCE YOUR CAR/ GET A NEW INSURANCE QUOTE.

"No room for Debt"

Cash Is King

Manage money, not debt

Like so many young people in college, we accepted our first credit card offer upon arriving at school. The credit card companies would give away free food if we would sign up for a credit card. And almost every college student knows that food is the hottest commodity on campus. So, when someone was giving out a large bag of M&Ms for the cost of our address and signature on a piece of paper, we felt foolish not to take their candy. Fortunately, we understood that credit cards were essentially loans that we had 30 days to pay back, so we avoided ringing up an insane amount of debt like so many of our friends. In fact, most of the time we would just cut up the cards as soon as they came in the mail. But we did keep a few cards just in case of emergencies.

Well, those cards eventually began to be used for more than just emergencies and before long, we simply used the credit cards for just about every purchase. We were careful with our purchases, and didn't go overboard while in college, but the habit of spending with credit was formed.

In our minds, there was no difference between the amount of money we spent when using cash or using credit cards. We were disciplined in our finances so our feeling was that the credit card simply made life easier. We didn't need to carry cash with us, and we even got perks for using the cards like airline miles or cash back on the credit card. So, for years we used credit cards as our main tool for purchasing until we began to see a troubling trend in our finances. We noticed that the amount of money we spent increased slowly over time and we began to go over budget every month. We would say to ourselves that we would cut back on spending, but every month it seemed as though we would spend more than we planned.

After some time, we began to recognize that we were not going to be able to stick to our budget unless we put some hard spending limits on ourselves. It was just too easy to swipe the credit card and forget about it. We decided to move to a cash budget. Except for things that we automatically pay such as mortgage, utilities, and our tithe to our church, we spend only cash! We made a commitment that we would take cash out of the bank for the amount we would budget for ourselves each month. We would only spend that money, and once the money was gone, it was gone! THAT WAS THE SOLUTION! We immediately were back on budget. The cash budget worked for three key reasons:

1. Cash forces the limit

Once the cash runs out, we don't have any ability to go over budget. We essentially put a wall up between ourselves and our money. This takes discipline. In the beginning, the urge to cheat was strong. We would run out of money and the thought to just use the credit card would creep up on us. But we recognized that once we broke down that wall it would be so much harder to put it back up. Truthfully, we did punch a few holes in the wall at times, and immediately felt as though we had failed - because we had! The next month, we built an even stronger wall. The key is that you must commit to sticking to the budget first and the cash just makes it easier to do so. Our failure was not with the cash budget itself, but with making a commitment to sticking to it.

2. Cash causes pain

Whenever we spend cash, we can visually see the money leaving our hand and the stack of cash that we have get smaller and smaller over time. With every spending motion, there is recognition that we are never going to have the tool back in our hand again. And, when that cash pile gets low, that recognition becomes a bit painful. If you think about it, that makes sense because when we purchase something, we are essentially exchanging one thing of value for another thing of value. We visually see the exchange, and our brain recognizes the loss and gain. Depending on whether we got a good deal or if we really needed the item we purchased, we feel good or bad about that transaction. With credit cards, there is no exchange. We are not physically giving anything away, so we don't really see the loss. We see only the gain of stuff. Perception becomes reality - a deceptive reality. We only see and feel the loss one time a month when we pay the credit card bill as opposed to seeing and feeling the loss every time we make a purchase

> ***...OUR FAILURE WASN'T WITH THE CASH BUDGET ITSELF, BUT WITH MAKING A COMMITMENT TO STICKING TO IT.***

with cash. That feeling of loss is what helps us limit our spending when we use cash. The lack of that feeling is why study after study shows that we spend more with credit cards.

3. Cash is a visual budget

When we use only cash, we can visually see when we are getting close to our budget. When the stack of money is large, we are doing well with the budget, especially when we have a lot of money at the end of the month. Similarly, when the stack of money is low, we know that we need to hold off on spending. We really don't need to look at our spreadsheet or do any calculations to figure out our financial situation, and that keeps budgeting simple.

So now, we answer the questions everyone is likely thinking: "Did you get rid of all of your credit cards? If so, how did you build your credit score?" The answer is no, we did not get rid of all our credit cards. We even pay most of our recurring bills on automatic payment with our credit cards, such as our cell phone and other utilities. We also set-up our credit card to be paid off completely from our bank account every month, so we **NEVER** pay any late fees or interest. However, we did not do this so that we could build our credit score. The truth of the matter is that your credit score is useful only when you are going to make a large purchase in which you will need a loan, such as when you want to buy a house or car, and you don't make those purchases very often. Plus, your credit score is based on all your debt, not just credit cards. By paying your rent, utilities, medical bills, etc. on time, you are building a great credit history, and a fixed limit credit card to help build your credit isn't bad **AS LONG AS YOU PAY IT OFF EVERY MONTH!** So, if you know you will not be able to restrain yourself from using the credit card outside of only those expenses, then you need to cut it up and get it as far away from your wallet as possible. But if you can put the card in your drawer and not use it - except for consistent bills - then use it that way.

The important thing to understand is to use cash for your day-to-day expenses such as food, entertainment, and clothes. By doing this, you will do just fine in sticking to your budget.

Recurring Bills

As we mentioned, we use our credit card to pay bills that occur monthly for the convenience. But we want to stress, once again, that we pay off that credit card 100% every month. All these bills are set up to get paid automatically and this is actually a very good way to manage our budget and our bills. Once you have used your cash for two months and you see how your bank account fluctuates as you pay your bills and spend your cash budget, you can set up your recurring bills to be paid automatically through your bank account or a credit card. Our recommendation would be that you do it from your bank account, however, if you choose to do it with a credit card, that is fine too. Just make sure it is setup to be paid off automatically from your bank account every month. By setting up your bills to be paid automatically, you will begin to feel the stress of paying bills go away. It may be stressful the first month because for the first time, you are not in direct control of the payment every month. But at the same time, you should feel the relief of not constantly trying to figure out whether you are going to have enough money to pay one bill or another. For as long as your income stays the same, you don't have any unexpected expenses, and you don't overspend your cash, you can be certain that your bills will be paid! That within itself should be a relief. You only need to check your bank account monthly to make sure nothing out of the ordinary has occurred and just relax.

...PAY OFF THAT CREDIT CARD 100% EVERY MONTH.

"Decisions...decisions"

Prioritize Spending

Buy what you need and get what you want

We all have done it before. Impulse buying! Whether it is the thing we just gotta have or it's the thing that's on sale, we all have purchased something that we wanted in the moment. Inevitably, not too long after we have it in our possession, we realize that we didn't really need it at all. A few years back, Dot and I made a commitment to getting back into shape.

We were going to start eating better and working out. We were committed to living a healthy lifestyle from that point on! For us to do that, we went out and signed up for a fitness center membership and bought a treadmill, some aerobic weights, a punching bag/mini boxing set-up, and all the work out gear to accompany our new lifestyle...I think you all know where this is going.

We worked out religiously for about two weeks, and then life happened. Between work, kids, church, and everything else we had going on in our lives, we did not have enough time to workout at the gym and did not have the energy to even workout at home. Before long, the treadmill was collecting dust, the workout clothes shifted to the back of the drawer, and the punching bag was swinging in the corner of the basement as a relic of what could have been.

Our problem was not the desire to be healthy; that actually is an excellent goal. The mistake we made was we thought a healthy lifestyle was going to be the main priority in our life going forward. In our enthusiasm, we neglected to think about all the other commitments we had that would eventually take priority over the healthy lifestyle we desired. Correctly prioritizing is a problem we all have at some point, and we mention it here because our understanding of our priorities effects our finances as well.

In our zeal for a healthy lifestyle and lack of understanding of our priorities, we quickly spent thousands of dollars that essentially amounted to nothing. Some would say that is no big deal because we had already learned to manage our budget well enough to know we could afford those things, but it is a problem for us and should be a problem for you whenever you waste money. Remember, money is a tool. You don't just throw useful tools away on an impulse or whim. A landscaper doesn't decide to just throw out a perfectly good lawnmower because he has two more. He uses that lawnmower for all its worth and sells it when he's done with it because, even then, it still has value. We shouldn't toss away money just because we can afford to lose it. We need to get all we can out of our tools.

What do you value?

So, how can we avoid throwing away our money? We can do that by thinking about what we really value in life and prioritizing our spending. We are not talking about the essentials of life here. Food, shelter, utilities, and emergency savings should, of course, be the highest priority for your money. However, when you make your budget, you might find that you have some money left over after the essentials, or, you may find that you spend money on things that you don't really value like fast food or entertainment. Once you prioritize your wants, you can cut back on the nonessential spending so that you can have some extra to spend on other things you really value.

The first thing you need to do is figure out what you value. We have found the easiest way to do that is to make a list. So, take one minute to make a list of the things you value. Then circle the three or four things that you value most. Your list may look something like the one below:

Time with Family

Buckeye Football

Golf

Watching Movies

Good Food

Traveling the World

Relationship with God

Helping People in Need

Relaxing by Myself

Spending Time with Friends

By identifying your values, you will learn a bit about yourself that maybe you didn't really realize before. Even more so, you will know where you should focus your spending to get the most out of your money. Using the list above you can justify spending money on buying a big screen TV to watch movies and football games, or, justify spending large sums of money to go on mission trips or vacations. In those cases, you would be spending money on things that you need while also getting what you want. We need to have the things that we value to have happiness in our lives. According to that list, it would not be good for us to spend money on a new iPad or go shopping at the department store just because there is a sale. If we were to spend our money on those things, we would get some things that *we want, but don't need*, and have to sacrifice something of higher value that we both want and need.

> ***...MONEY IS A TOOL. YOU DON'T JUST THROW USEFUL TOOLS AWAY ON AN IMPULSE OR WHIM.***

In a perfect world, we would be able to spend unlimited money on everything that we value. But, in the real world, we must choose where and how we spend. By prioritizing our values, we can spend our resources where we are going to get the most satisfaction and avoid spending on things we don't really need or want. Ultimately, by making these decisions, we will have more happiness in our lives and, at the same time, be financially secure.

"....a solid foundation"

Building Wealth

Investing 101

Okay, so you now have a good idea of how to spend your money well. Now, we are going to talk about how you can use your money to make money for you. You see, a good job and income will get you out of poverty, and proper budgeting will keep you out of poverty, but, you will not reach a point of financial comfort until your money begins making money.

This is the practice of building wealth. Just so you know, this is NOT how you get rich quick! In fact, it is quite the opposite. This is the "get rich slow" method - the only true way to ensure wealth without hitting the lottery or marrying into money! Of course, if you have the chance to marry into money, go for it! Basically, if you follow our advice on this, you will be able to retire without needing to worry about money when you get older, and maybe even have some extra to give away, if you desire.

Savings

The first step to building wealth is to start a savings account. This is too important to pass up! You must, must, must have a savings account. In fact, you need two savings accounts.

1) Savings Account #1 - You need the first account so that you can have some money put away for emergencies. There is no doubt that your car is going to break down or something in your house will break. And, whether you like it or not, you are going to have some major unexpected expense hit you from out of nowhere. IT IS GOING TO HAPPEN! So, instead of acting like it's not going to happen, you should prepare for it to happen. So, how much should you save? Our advice - save $500 as fast as you can to cover any immediate emergencies. This may take a month or two but do whatever it takes. Sell a kidney or

rake leaves in the neighborhood... just kidding about that kidney, but you get the point. Get that $500! After you have the $500 in your savings account, you should save at least $50/month every month until you die! Yep, you heard right. You put that money away now and when you have that unexpected expense come up, you can dig into this savings account and pay for it. When you have this kind of savings account, you know that you don't have to worry about how you will pay for emergencies. You have prepared for them! That is no-financial-stress living.

2) Saving Account #2 - You actually start this account after the first savings account and after you invest in your employer's 401K, but it felt right to include this information here, so you aren't surprised later. Don't worry, we will summarize the order at the end of this chapter. This partic-

WHETHER YOU LIKE IT OR NOT, YOU ARE GOING TO HAVE SOME MAJOR UNEXPECTED EXPENSE HIT YOU FROM OUT OF NO-WHERE

ular savings account is for quick-access wealth building. The goal is that you will not spend this money for a long period of time. It can be used as a super safety net if you have some emergency expense that is greater than your first savings account can handle, but, prayerfully, that never happens. Think of this account as a holding account for your big, money-making investments. The amount you put into this account should be about 5% of your take-home check. Meaning, if you bring home $1000/week, you should be putting $50/week into this account. Once this account reaches $5000 you should shift that 5% into a long-term investment account (we will discuss in the next section). Your options for this money are endless, but we suggest that you let it grow in a savings account that you can always access, if needed. And, when the time comes, you can use the money as part of a down payment on your house. Now, this may not be enough to cover your full down payment, but it will help.

When you get extra money from your tax return or a bonus from work, you should use that kind of income to build these savings accounts as well.

Long-Term Investments

Once you have your savings accounts setup and you are putting money into those accounts, you should begin investing into long-term accounts. That is when your money really starts working for you. Two of these long-term accounts invest money into the stock market, where you will buy pieces of companies (called "shares") and as those companies make money, you will make money as well. You will essentially be part-owner of the companies in which you invest.

For simplicity, we are only going to talk about three long-term investments: 401K, 529Plan, and housing. There are many other options, but the truth is, if you are able to max out these investment options, then you are making that really big money and you might need to consider hiring a professional money manager or working with a financial advisor. If that is the case, be sure to talk with people you trust to recommend a good advisor. After managing our own money and investments for over 20 years, we finally decided to find an investor so that we could take advantage of the different tax codes that surround certain investments. We use Thrivent Financial, because we share common values with their organization and our advisor. Just so you know, they did not pay us to mention them in our book. Again, you only need to worry about this after you have at least 2 savings accounts, a 401k Plan, 529 Plan, and you own your home.

1) 401K - A 401K account is a long-term investment account that usually is run by your employer. The money you put into the ac-

count is invested into the stock market. Often in your company, but you can choose the type of investment you prefer in the account. We suggest investing in index mutual funds that mirror the whole stock market. So, when the stock market is going up, you are making money. When it is going down, don't worry about it. It will go back up soon enough. This is the basic, yet essential long-term investment. If you don't already have this setup at your job, you need to do so right away. A 401K is the best investment tool out there for you because often your employer will match the amount of money you put into this investment. In addition, the government will not tax that money. Essentially, you get free money when you put money into your 401K. That truly is having your money make money! We believe that you should be putting at least 5% of your pre-taxed income in your 401K plan. So, if you are making $50,000 a year, you should plan to start investing $2500 a year into your 401K and once your second savings account reaches $5000, you should then start putting 10% of your income into this account. Now, consider that your job will likely match 2-4% of your income into this account for free. If you follow those steps, then you would retire with over $456,000 after 25yrs!!! To get to that number, we calculated investment growth at 7% per year. And we didn't even include your possibilities for raises and promotions, so our calculated number is likely lower than the actual amount. If you're 25 now, you could be retired at 50! We do not recommend retiring that young, but you could. What are you waiting for? Get started on this right now!

2) 529 Plan - The 529 Plan is a college savings plan that uses stock investments to grow, just like your 401k. Now, you may be thinking, "Why am I thinking about saving for college?" Well, the truth of the matter is that real wealth is not built in one generation. Think about it; real money is inherited and passed down from generation to generation. We want you to start thinking about building wealth for your children and grandchildren now. **Note**: This is not just so that you can be a blessing to your children. That is a great thing by itself. But by investing in your children, you also are investing in yourself. Here's how:

A. Protecting your investment - If your children go to college, they likely will earn good money on their own and will not need to beg you for money when they are grown. Never thought of that, huh?

B. Increasing your investment - If you ensure your kids go to college, they most likely will earn good money and be able to bless you once they are making good money! And what if they end up doing something spectacular like becoming the next Elon Musk or Bill Gates?! Then, you too, strike it rich because you invested in your child. You smell what we're cookin'?

C. Good, Cheap Housing - At some point in time, you are going to be too old to live alone. Wouldn't it be nice to be able to live with your children and grandchildren? When they are making good money, you can use some of your retirement to build an extra room or even a full apartment onto their house. This is A LOT cheaper than assisted living, and you get to be around family. Plus, they would have live-in babysitting, which would be cheaper for them as well. This is just plain genius, right...? All you gotta do is help get them through college and your money is truly making money for you and them! P.S. Relationships with your kids will always matter and will make a big difference in whether this housing invest-

...BY INVESTING IN YOUR CHILDREN YOU ARE ALSO INVESTING IN YOURSELF.

ment will work for you or not. Be sure to wisely work on building those relationships as well.

You can invest in a 529 Plan through several different methods. You can look on-line to find one that works for you in your state. A perk to this investment is that you get a state tax deduction for all the money you put into a 529 Plan. You should get a separate 529 Plan for each of your children and we recommend putting at least $50/mo, per child, in there. If you can afford to do more, definitely do more. Our eldest son started college in 2017 and we have been putting $200/mo into his account for at least 8 years. We still will not have enough saved to cover all his college, but we have more than we would have had if we had not invested anything at all. You also can ask family and friends to put money into their 529 account instead of giving them excessive and expensive birthday/Christmas presents. Again, your money is making money.

3) Buy a house - You need to first get your savings going and your 401K plan. After you have those moving and you see that you have enough resources to properly fund those, you should consider buying a house.

We bought our first home after only being out of college and married for 2 years. We purchased it for about $140K. It was a nice home in a good school district. We took out a 30-yr mortgage and had almost no money to put down. And to top it off, we had just had our first child. Needless to say, we were in no financial shape to purchase a home outside of having two steady incomes. However, after only living in the house for 3 years, we were able to sell it for more than what we paid for it, and, as a result, had a little bit of money to put down on our second home. Despite making several errors in the purchase contract, we still were able to come out on top. ***#readALL-thefineprint***

You see, a home gives you an investment that, over time, nine times out of ten, will increase in value...as long as you take care of the house. You should only buy a house that you can afford. A good rule of thumb is this: The sum of your mortgage, insurance, and taxes should be the same as the amount you are willing to pay in rent. Realtors will tell you to buy a house that cost 3 times what you make in a year. **That is garbage!** We believe a house that costs 2 times your annual salary is a better target – remember, this is coming to you as a loan. Being house-poor is real! So, if you make $75,000 a year, your house should cost no more than $150,000. You should also plan on living in the house for at least 7 years in order to make any money (a.k.a. equity) when you sell the house. Purchase a house that you would like to live in for some time and then you can upgrade once you are making more money. We also recommend that you take out a 10- or 15-year mortgage on the house so you can pay it off faster and get more money when you sell it. That is a great investment because a lot of the money you would have paid in rent, you will get back when you sell the house, and any money you don't get back (i.e., Interest paid on the mortgage and the taxes) will be eligible for a tax deduction. Again, this is your money, making money for you.

One final recommendation for when you are thinking about purchasing your house: Save 20% of the cost of the house in cash so that you don't get hit with an extra payment called PMI (Private Mortgage Insurance). We didn't do this on our first home and paid over $1000/yr more than needed. PMI is an extra charge for people who cannot put down enough money. Most people think that is just part of buying a house - **it's not!** It's basically a poor-person's fee. At a minimum, you should have 10% to put down in cash and then in a year or two have your house appraised to see if you can have the PMI expense taken off because of the equity in the home. We don't want to get too deep into equity and home values, but look into it on your own, especially if you already own your home and are paying PMI.

Life Insurance

Life Insurance isn't really a long-term investment in the sense that it gains value over time, but it is a way to make sure your family can continue building wealth if you were to have an accident and die prematurely. We know that no one likes to think about death, but it is irresponsible to not prepare for it just in case. Personally, we both know that if one of us were to die, it would be extremely hard for the other to continue to build wealth on their own, not even considering the emotional toll it would take. So, to make sure that we secure one another's financial futures in the case of an untimely death, we both have life insurance policies, and we have one another along with our children as the beneficiaries. We recommend you do the same. We also recommend that you have different policies based on your stage in life, but ONLY TERM policies, which pay only upon death. Do not buy a life insurance policy connected to any type of investment. Universal life insurance or variable universal life insurance, etc., are not good policies. Just buy straight term life insurance. Here are some recommendations based on your life situation:

Single no Children: We recommend that you buy a policy that will cover your funeral cost. That will usually be about $10-$15,000! Yes, funerals are EXPENSIVE. Check with your employer because they may offer small policies like this at a low cost. If you have a church or special charity that you are passionate about, you also can get a slightly larger policy so that you can donate money to them. But mostly, you just want to make sure your parents or siblings don't have to come out-of-pocket for your funeral. They will love you all the more for that!

One dependent (Either married w/o children or you have only one child): We recommend that you multiply your income by 5 years and purchase that amount of term life insurance. So, if you make $50,000/year you need a $250,000 life insurance policy. That is not enough money to change your surviving spouse's/child's lifestyle, but it will give them relief so that as they grieve your loss, they don't also have to lose everything that you wanted for them.

More than one dependent (Either Married with children or more than one child): We recommend that you multiply your income by 10 years and purchase that amount of term life insurance. This will take care of your family for some time and make sure that your children will be able to attend college and maybe even have a down payment for their own homes. In doing that, you are setting a foundation for generational wealth and your family will remember what you did for them even in your absence.

We cannot stress enough how important it is to start building your wealth now. The earlier you start saving and investing, the faster your wealth grows. Many people don't think about doing these things and therefore, never get a chance to retire, or, they live paycheck to paycheck for their entire lives. You can do better than that! We know that you can because you have gotten this far in the book, so you're definitely serious about being financially secure for the rest of your life.

Quick Review

To recap, here is the order of things we've said that you need to do in order to start building wealth:

1. Save $500 as soon as possible and then save $50/mo 'till you die! For emergency expenses!
2. Put 5% of your check go into your 401K at work.
3. Start putting 5% of your take-home pay into a 2nd Savings Account until you save $5000
4. Increase your 401K contribution to 10% of your check. If this is scary, put in at least as much as your company matches and work your way up to 10%
5. Start a 529 Plan for each of your children
6. Buy a house
7. Buy term life insurance

THE FIRST STEP TO BUILDING WEALTH IS TO START A SAVINGS ACCOUNT. THIS IS TOO IMPORTANT TO PASS UP.

"...coming out the woodwork!"

Last Things First

Stuff You Gotta Know

There are a few additional things we want to lay out for you that are important. We do not want to go too deep, though, because we would end up writing a whole separate book! However, we believe that you need to know these things as well...

1) Don't Throw It Away

Now that you have a little bit of money, people are

going to try to get you to invest in either some crazy "get rich quick" scheme, or a business idea that they have. The best advice we have is to simply smile and say, "No thanks. That is not for me." You know that 99% of the time, the only way to make more money is through hard work and patience. So, when someone tells you that you should "become a partner" or "all you have to do is sign up 10 people," etc... know that it's a hustle. Most of those are pyramid schemes where a few people at the top are making money and you are at the bottom giving them your money. Just know that there is no such thing as "passive income" when you must do anything more than invest your money. The next time someone tells you to invest in something, pay for training, and then you can sell a product or service for passive income after you get other people to sign up under you...just know you are being suckered. I don't care how many people they show you that are making thousands of dollars now because they worked the system...it is a hustle and chances are people like you are making them that money. Your monthly fees, your training costs, you buying the products, and going to conferences all are putting the money in their pockets.

The same goes for friends or business people you may meet that have great ideas to start a restaurant, beauty/barber shop, build an app, or whatever. If you are willing to take the time to work side-by-side with them to make that business work, then perhaps you might take that into consideration. However, nine times out of ten, the reason that their business idea is still only in the "idea" phase is because they don't have the ability to build it and, therefore, you likely will be throwing your money away along with theirs.

2) Relationships

There are two things we need to cover regarding relationships as they relate to money.

A. Two Incomes are better than one

It's obvious that when you have two people earning money in one household you will be more financially stable than a single income household. There is a reason why the majority of households that live in poverty are headed by single mothers.[2] This is because it is just terribly hard to keep money and almost impossible to build wealth as a single person. Therefore, if you are serious about building wealth, you should be thinking about marriage sooner than later. Yep, we went there! The numbers don't lie. If you want financial stability, then you should not fall into the mindset that you need to discover yourself first or that you must find Miss Perfect or Mr. Wonderful. Instead, come to the realization you are who you are and start looking for Mrs. Pays Her Bills on Time/Not Crazy and Mr. Nice Guy with a Solid Work History/Right Priorities. Honestly, if you can be their friend, then you can build a life together and a

2 https://www.federalsafetynet.com/us-poverty-statistics.html

stable financial life at that!

Being single and liking to mingle is not a good financial move and living together without the firm commitment that comes with marriage is unstable. You are more likely to leave that relationship with a greater financial responsibility, such as children/ child support, and a tough financial situation. And because we have already gone there, it's hard to find a good marriage candidate who wants the additional financial liability of children. It's not impossible, many with children get married, but it is often harder. We are not passing judgement if you find yourself trying to build wealth as a single parent or you are paying child support. Especially if you are single as a result of divorce. That is a hard situation in which to recover. You are doing the right thing by using this book to get your finances in order. We are simply stating the fact that it is more difficult to build financial wealth as an individual.

Dot and I got together as teenagers with the goal of getting out of poverty because we knew two incomes were better than one and we fell in love over time. All we knew of each other at the time of our agreement was that she wasn't crazy, and I was a nice guy. We were both sick and tired of being poor and everything else fell into place. Think about it....just sayin'.

B) Family Borrowing Money

Family relationships can be difficult. Now that you have some financial security, you likely have already had family members come and ask you for money. If it hasn't happened yet...just wait for it. There are two ways that we recommend handling this:

1. Don't loan money...Give money. If a family member is asking you for a loan there is a good chance they are not currently managing their money well, which means that there is little to no chance that you are going to get your money back. When they don't pay it back, you will be upset with them and the relationship will suffer. Thanksgiving dinner and Christmas will be really weird, and it just spirals downhill from there. We have learned this the hard way! We have "loaned" many thousands of dollars to family and friends over the years and we can remember only three occasions when we were actually repaid any amount of that money. Now, when people ask, we simply ask ourselves how much money we are willing to give and we provide that amount. Depending on the person and circumstance, we may tell them it is a gift and ask them not to return it, or we may tell them to give it back to us when they are able so that they don't feel like a charity case. Even then, we have no expectations of them paying it back.

2. Give so they don't come back. At times, people will ask us for money more than once even though they have not returned or even thought about the first amount that we "loaned" them. These situations are real problems because you know that the person is not going to pay you back, and

there is a good chance that if they asked twice, they would ask a third and fourth time. If we tell them "no" we know that it will hurt the relationship and depending on who the person is, we may not want to do that. As a couple, we have decided that when they ask, we will give them a sizable amount of money based on what we can afford at that time. That way, they will not be able to forget nor act like it didn't happen. Hence, they usually will not ask for money again because they know that we have already helped them out in a big way.

> ***DON'T LOAN MONEY...GIVE MONEY.***

3) Giving

While dealing with family is hard, we try our best to give if someone has a need. However, we don't want to create a situation where we are ATM machines for family members who have not learned to manage their finances. We do the things we have outlined above, but at the same time, we want to give to people, family or not, who experience hard times. Our preference is to give through our church. We believe that everything that we have is a blessing from God and our response to this blessing is to set aside 10% to give back to God through His church. We did not always feel that way, but once we started to give, we found that we didn't miss the money at all. Of course, like every amount of money that we spend or give away, we plan for it in our budget, so we know how much we are going to give. One thing that we have noticed is that as we give, we also see ourselves save more and need to spend less. We consider this a second blessing from God. So, if you are a Christ-follower we encourage you to put this in your budget as well. We are certain you will see similar results to ours.

If you are not a Christ-follower, we still encourage you to set aside money to give away for the benefit of others who are less financially well-off. Helping others will give you more joy than buying that new thing you want.

We have not yet met anyone who's been generously giving and tithing and has not felt better about themselves and about how they manage their finances. Another perk we've observed and experienced through our generosity is that we will feel less guilt about telling our family members, "No." We believe you will feel the same.

4) Catch Bad Decisions Early

You are going to make some financial errors in life. Buying that gym membership that you don't use, making a bad investment, purchasing a junk car that didn't work out so well are the kinds of things that are going to happen. The best thing you can do is learn from those situations and make the changes needed to not continue to lose money. Cancel the unused memberships and subscriptions right away. Don't continue to pay for them if you are not getting your money's worth. Cut your losses and move on.

You also can return items that you know were bad purchasing decisions. This is not the same as buying a dress, wearing it, and then returning it. That is stealing! We are talking about returning items that you bought on a whim and regretted purchasing them almost as soon as you got home. Return the item(s) and don't think twice about it.

5) Learn to spend less

There are so many ways to avoid spending money.

- Use the sharing economy - there are dozens of online groups that will allow you to exchange goods for services. People often give away furniture or appliances that they no longer want and all you need to do is pick them up.
- Use the library - Books, movies, newspapers, magazines are all available at the Library. They also offer free internet service so you can save money there if needed.
- Use Coupons - We don't suggest that you try to start "couponing" like the folks who learn to game the system and get $100s of dollars worth of items for next to nothing. We think that's insane because the amount of time used to find those coupons (and it's a lot of time) can be used work-

ing a second job. In addition, with those insane couponing schemes, you often can buy only odds and ends like off brand deodorant or diet sports drinks. We suggest you clip coupons from various legit sources (your local newspaper or online) for items you were already going to buy. So, make your list first and then see if you can find a coupon to match.

- Free amenities in your city - Look for opportunities to go to free events in your city as a fun outing instead of paying for a night out. Concerts in the park, museums, and similar events are often available and you only need to look for them (online search engines are a great for that).
- Ask for a discount - You never know when there is a sale going on and you just didn't get the memo. If you have a nice salesclerk, they may just apply the latest coupon even though you don't have it with you. Most people are good people, and you never know when their kindness can benefit your bottom line.
- Turn down the thermostat - You can save at least $20 dollars a month on utility bills by just changing your temperature a few degrees. We keep our heat on 68 degrees during the day in the winter and tell everyone to put on a sweater if they are cold. We allow it to drop down to 64 degrees at night because everyone is asleep and never knows the difference. In the summer, we keep the AC at

78 degrees and allow it to go up to 82 degrees at night...again...you don't care when you're sleeping. Our gas and electric bills are a lot less than our friends and families despite our house often being bigger. We probably save $500 a year on utilities. Over the last 20 years, that's $10,000 in our pockets, or better yet, in our investments earning real "passive income".

...A HOME GIVES YOU AN INVESTMENT THAT, OVER TIME, NINE TIMES OUT OF TEN WILL INCREASE IN VALUE...AS LONG AS YOU TAKE CARE OF IT.

"Piece of Cake!!! It's all in the abs!"

Wrapping it Up

Summing it up in a few points

1) Money is a tool

- Don't get emotionally attached to money. It's just a tool to buy stuff!

2) Make a budget

- Know how much money you have coming in and how much you spend. Spend less than you make! It really is that simple.

3) Cash is King

- Spend only cash. If you use a credit card, then always pay it off in full at the end of the month. If you can't pay it off in full every month, then you should not have a credit card - period!

4)Get Your Priorities Straight

- Don't spend money on things that don't really matter. Know what is important to you and only spend money on those things. You will regret purchasing everything else. Avoid buyer's remorse!

5)Make Your Money Make Money

- Build an emergency savings account and a regular savings account. Invest in your 401k at work. Invest in your kid's 529 Plan; then buy a house. Get some life insurance just in case.

6)Stuff You Gotta Know

- Get married for the money (and for love). Don't fall for get-rich-quick schemes. Just give money to your family, don't loan it. Save money wherever you can.

That covers it! Living a life where financial stress is a thing of the past is not too hard to do. It does take effort and some planning, but it definitely is not rocket science. You probably have already overcome the odds by breaking out of a bad financial situation.

Ensuring you do not end up back there should be a lot easier for you than getting out was. If you stick to the plan presented in this book, you will have no problems building wealth for yourself and for generations to come.

Appendix A

FINANCIAL LOG

DATE	DESCRIPTION	CATEGORY	AMOUNT
Total			

Categories
Housing (Rent, mortgage, taxes, insurance)
Transportation (Gas, Bus, Car Note, Repairs)
Utilities (Gas, Electric)
Telephone
Groceries
Medical
Dining, travel, entertainment (Including Cable, Netflix)
Debt payments
Clothing
Savings
Education
Charity
Miscellaneous

Appendix B

FINANCIAL LOG

DATE	DESCRIPTION	CATEGORY	AMOUNT
1/2	Rent	Housing	$775.00
1/2	Kroger	Groceries	$45.34
1/3	Kroger	Groceries	$17.87
1/3	McDonald	Dining	$8.74
1/4	Starbucks Card	Dining	$20.00
1/5	Leclead	Utilities	$103.39
1/5	Sprint	Telephone	$78.93
1/5	Chik-Fil-A	Dining	$21.66
1/7	Quick Trip	Gas/Transportation	$23.16
1/8	Meijer	Groceries	$12.35
1/8	Bath and Body	Misc	$7.69
1/8	Journey	Clothing	$54.89
1/9	BW-3s	Dining	$36.06
1/11	Tithes	Charity	$100.00
1/12	Wendy's	Dining	$5.15
1/15	Starbucks Card	Dining	$20.00
1/16	Ameren	Utilities	$60.00
1/16	Quick Trip	Transportation	$22.73
1/16	Jakes' Chrysler - Car Note	Transportation	$389.38
1/17	Kroger	Groceries	$41.63
1/19	Joe's Barbershop	Misc	$18.00
1/20	Progressive	Transportation	$212.44
1/23	Fitworks	Misc	$10.00
1/24	Quick Trip	Transportaion	$32.78
1/26	Kroger	Groceries	$82.70
1/26	Chick-Fil-A	Dining	$35.37
1/27	SoFi Credit	Education	$125.00
1/28	Peoples Church	Charity	$100.00
1/28	Chase Master Card	Debt	$125.00
1/28	Kids A Lot - Daycare	Education	$500.00
1/29	Papa Johns	Dining	$22.78
1/29	Starbucks Card	Dining	$20.00
1/30	Netflix	Entertainment	$33.79
1/30	Apple Music	Entertinment	$14.99
TOTAL			$3176.82

Sample Budget

Categories	Totals	Budget
Housing	$775.00	$775.00
Transportation	$680.49	$680.00
Utilities	$163.39	$165.00
Telephone	$78.93	$80.00
Groceries	$189.00	$200.00
Medical	$0.00	$0.00
Dining, Travel, Entertainment	$248.86	$75.00
Debt Payments	$125.00	$125.00
Clothing/Household	$54.89	$50.00
Savings	$0.00	$0.00
Education/Childcare	$625.00	$625.00
Charity (Church Offerings)	$200.00	$200.00
Miscellaneous	$36.26	$20.00
Total Expense	$3,176.82	$2,995.00

Appendix D

Income minus Expense Table

	Current Income-Expense	Budget
Total Income	$3384.71	$0.00
Total Expense	$3137.14	$0.00
Extra Money	$247.57	$0.00

Made in the USA
Monee, IL
04 November 2026

67365978R00049